Keeping Well

Leon Read

W
FRANKLIN WATTS
LONDON • SYDNEY

Contents

Look out for Tiger on the pages of this book. Sometimes he is hiding.

We can do lots of things to keep well.

Five-a-day

We need to eat a well-balanced diet.

This includes five fruits or vegetables a day.

Which foods do you eat?

stew and dumplings

pizza and chips

chicken and rice

pasta

Make your own favourite pretend food like this.

Brushing teeth

We need to look after our teeth.

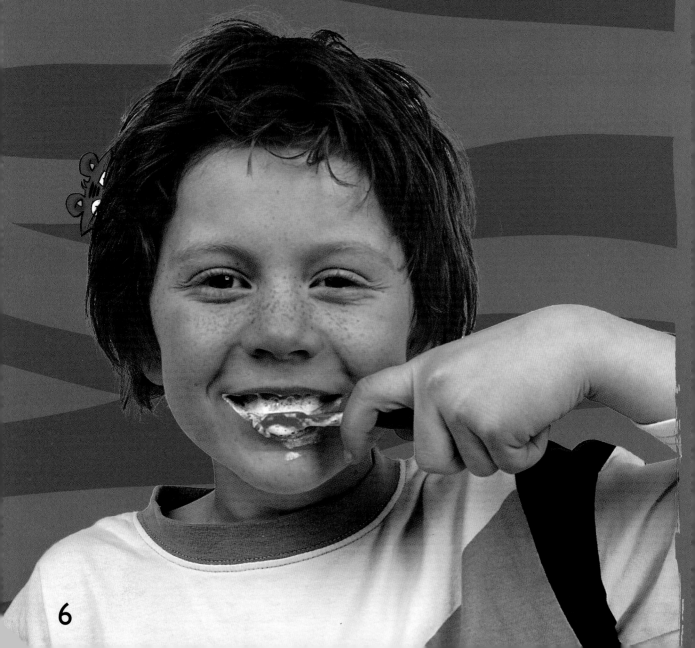

Brush your teeth twice a day
to keep them clean.

When was the last
time you saw
a dentist?

7

Good exercise

Exercise makes us strong.

We exercise by:

skipping...

dancing...

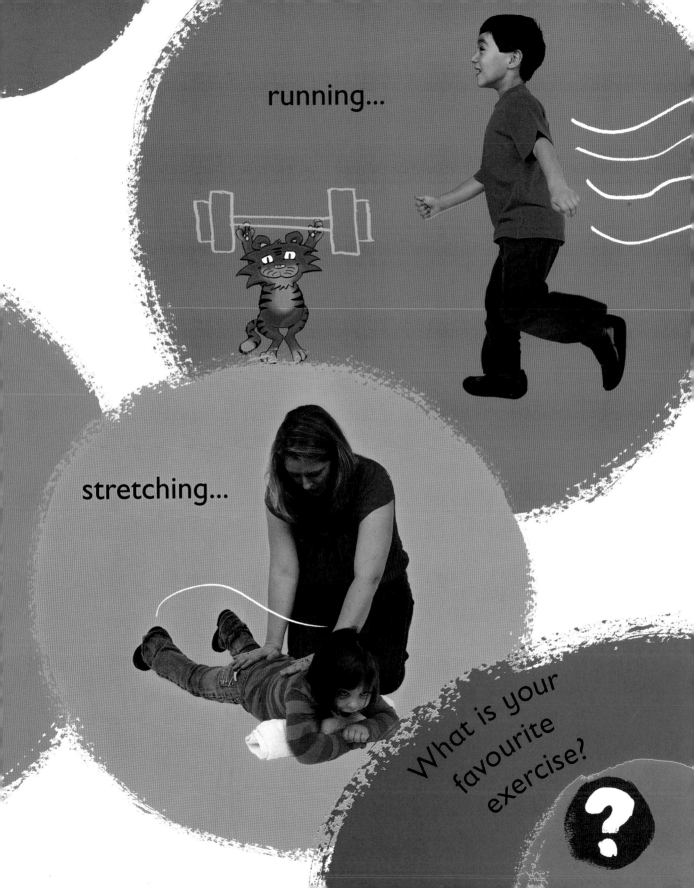

Washing hands

Before we eat we wash our hands to get rid of dirt and germs.

Feeling ill

Germs can make us ill. Germs are tiny.
We can only see them using a machine.

a real germ

I'm making a picture of a germ.

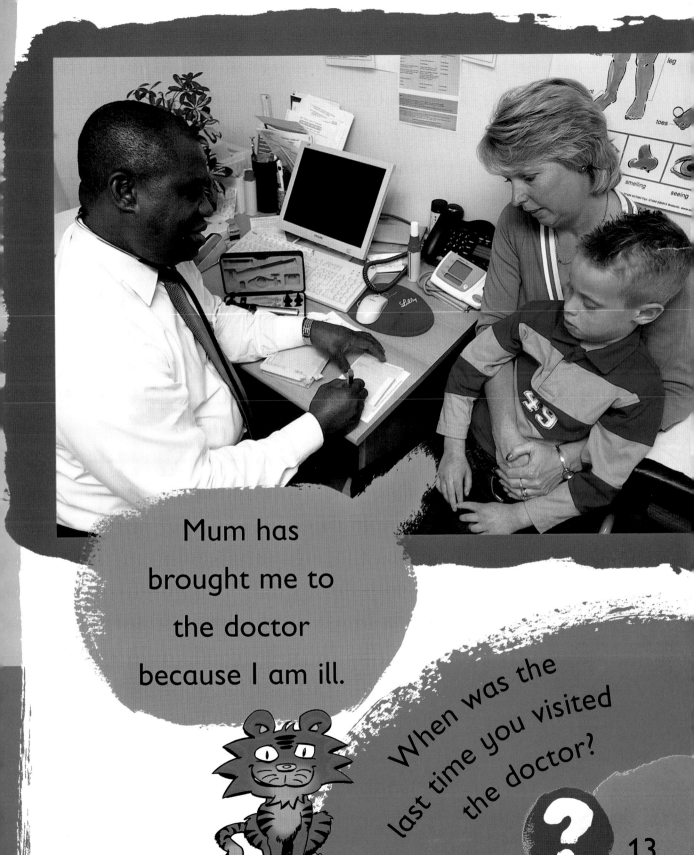

Mum has brought me to the doctor because I am ill.

When was the last time you visited the doctor?

13

Taking medicine

Sometimes we need medicine to make us better.

Tiger feels ill.

Only adults are allowed to give medicine.

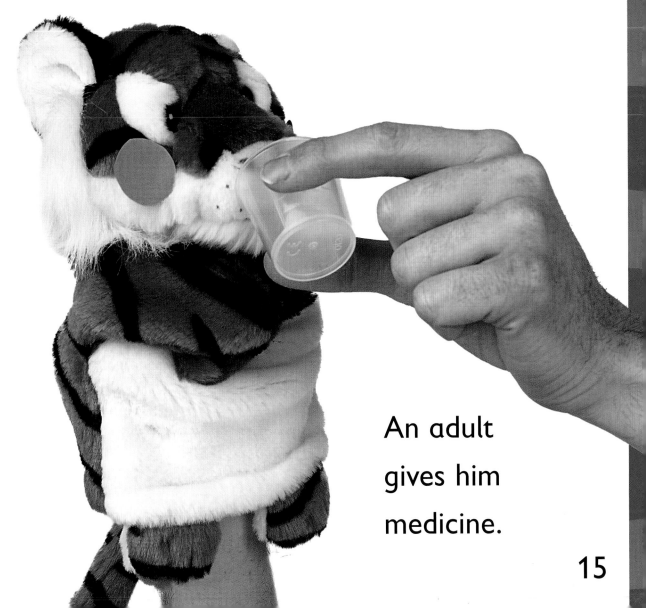

An adult gives him medicine.

What a mess!

Help to keep things clean
and tidy. Germs like mess.

I help my
dad clean up.

Look! Lucy has tripped over.

Why should Lucy tidy her bedroom?

Bath time!

Imagine what would happen
if you did not wash.

You would stink!

We read a story
about a frog
who didn't
want to wash.

Frog and the Bath

Sue Graves and Daniel Howarth

What other ways can you keep clean?

Time for bed

Everyone needs sleep. Without sleep we get tired and ill.

I like sleeping and dreaming.

What do you dream about when you sleep?

What time do you go to bed?

Feeling great

There are lots of different things we can do to keep well.

Adam is in a muddle.

Help him remember how to keep well.

What do I need to do before I eat food?

Why do I need to sleep?

Why do I need to exercise?

Why do I need to tidy my bedroom?

Word picture bank

Dentist – P. 7

Doctor – P. 13

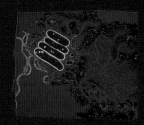

Germs – PP. 10, 12, 16

Pasta – P. 5

Skipping – P. 8

Wash – P. 19

First published in 2007 by Franklin Watts
338 Euston Road, London NW1 3BH

Franklin Watts Australia
Level 17/207 Kent Street, Sydney NSW 2000

Copyright © Franklin Watts 2007

Series editor: Adrian Cole
Photographer: Andy Crawford (unless otherwise credited)
Design: Sphere Design Associates
Art director: Jonathan Hair
Consultants: Prue Goodwin and Karina Law

A CIP catalogue record for this book is available
from the British Library.

ISBN: 978 0 7496 7614 8

Dewey Classification: 613

Acknowledgements:
The Publisher would like to thank Norrie Carr model agency
and Scope. 'Tiger' puppet used with kind permission from
Ravensden PLC (www.ravensden.co.uk).
Tiger Talk logo drawn by Kevin Hopgood.

Dr Linda Stannard/UCT/SPL (12tl, 24tr). Katherine
Fawssett/Image Bank/Getty Images (19bc).

Every attempt has been made to clear copyright.
Should there be any inadvertent omission
please apply to the publisher for rectification.

Printed in China

Franklin Watts is a division
of Hachette Children's Books,
an Hachette Livre UK company.

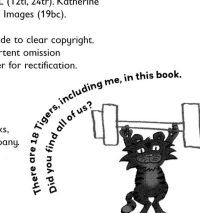

There are 18 Tigers, including me, in this book.
Did you find all of us?